MONEY MAGIC

Daily Journal To Successfully Manifest Wealth & Abundance Using The Law Of Attraction

First published in 2018 by Erin Rose Publishing

Text and illustration copyright © 2018 Erin Rose Publishing

Design: Julie Anson

ISBN: 978-1-911492-27-6

A CIP record for this book is available from the British Library.

MONEY MAGIC

Welcome to your Money Magic Journal!

You can become a money magnet and manifest greater wealth, prosperity and abundance by using the powerful yet simple techniques in this book.

The magic lies in the 3 keys to manifesting which can be used to attract money and abundance or whatever else you desire! So, if you are ready to use the power of positive thinking and the Law of Attraction you can dive right in and have fun creating the life you want to live.

Using the Law of Attraction and completing this guided daily journal, you can harness your power to fill up your bank account and boost your finances. You can start by using this journal as a fun workbook and 'play' with your creativity. Positive thinking is essential for this process and having fun literally raises your vibration and revitalises your energy, bringing you more of the same.

This daily journal helps you focus your energy on what you wish to achieve and guides you towards manifesting the life you dream of. It's natural to experience doubts but you'll learn how to upgrade your thoughts and maintain a positive mind-set using the powerful abundance affirmations. The power of positive thinking and the Law of Attraction can be used in all aspects of your life, including career, relationships, happiness and health. This journal is dedicated to attracting more money, wealth, prosperity and achieving greater abundance in your life.

Let's start creating the life you want to live!

The 3 Keys To Manifesting

Positivity elevates your energy and transforms your mood. When you radiate positivity it manifests in your experiences. The vibration of your entire energy system, thoughts, words, beliefs (including subconscious) and behaviour radiate out into the universe like a beacon of all that you are. Every thought, word and deed creates a flow of energy.

To master your manifestations, activate dynamic change by sending out powerful energy waves carrying your intention which return with your heart's desire.

Powerful manifesting is directly related to taking action and it is the most overlooked step in attaining what you truly want. If you have felt unable to manifest what you desire, could it be that activation was missing? It's like writing a letter and never posting it. When your energy is completely aligned and the 3 keys to manifesting are complete you can trust that what you ask for is on its way.

The **3 keys** are simple, powerful and essential.

🗝 **Intention**

🗝 **Energy**

🗝 **Action**

Using them step by step and aligning your intentions creates big shifts and real manifestations.

🔑 Intention

Step 1 is setting your intention. Firstly, clear some space, breathe deeply and relax. Setting your intention is making a clear, positive statement to manifest your desired outcome. Be specific about exactly what it is that you want, why you want it and when. Feel powerful and confident when you set your intention, knowing you have the power to create whatever you desire. Whatever you wish for, make the wise intention that it is for your own or someone else's greater good and adding 'this or something better' will prevent limitations.

🔑 Energy

Step 2 is committing your energy. Visualise yourself manifesting your goal. Feel the emotions when you receive it. Picture the scene. Really feel into it. Sense every little detail. Take your time and let the energy build up until it feels powerful and real. Lock in your intention with the Universe, trusting it is already manifesting.

🔑 Action

Step 3 is making a physical movement to release your intention. The action can be as simple as breathing out long and hard, sending your wish out in your breath. You can pretend to throw an intention-filled energy ball containing your wish or wave the air away from you with your hand, wafting your intention into the Universe. Enjoy this part, be creative in sending out your wish and have fun with it. If you feel silly, remind yourself action enforces your intention.

If you move the air you move the energy. It's about feeling and being in the flow. When you feel the flow you can trust the life force in and around you. In Tai Chi you'll see internal and external forces of energy together in movement. Physically moving the energy fully activates your intention and completes the process. When you believe, it is already real.

Another form of action is taking daily steps towards your goal. It encourages opportunities when you demonstrate you are ready, active and willing to receive. So, whether it's sending an email, researching websites, networking or talking to a friend, take action towards your desire. If you aren't sure what steps to take, look for coincidences and signposts as you are shown which direction to take.

Checking For Blocks To Manifesting

Blocks to manifesting do exist and often when we feel resistance it's because of a self-sabotaging belief, such as a belief that it's greedy to want more money or perhaps you were brought up to believe money was bad or that you aren't deserving of prosperity.

Try to recognise if you have low level thoughts of disbelief and negativity and take steps to nip them in the bud. It's worth digging a bit deeper to find out what your real beliefs are about money, security, abundance or your ability to have what you really desire.

On a sheet of paper, write down all the beliefs and feelings you have about money and abundance. Are there any fear-based beliefs lurking subconsciously? What would happen if you had more money? Perhaps you heard negativity from your family about money when you were growing up. If any negative beliefs surface, you can use an affirmation to dissolve it.

For instance, self-esteem issues, beliefs in lack of wealth and poverty thinking can sabotage you, so using an affirmation such as 'I am worthy and deserving of wealth.'

There are positive abundance affirmations provided, or you can create your own to help clear any self-sabotaging beliefs and feelings which may be blocking you from manifesting what you truly desire. Some blocks can be cleared instantly, depending on how deeply held the negative beliefs are and sometimes you have to fake it until you make it! Eventually positive thoughts and beliefs become your reality.

Make A Wish List

You can have fun creating your wish list below which will help you focus on what you want you wish to manifest. Empty your wishes, thoughts and desires onto the page below and brainstorm what you'd like to attain.

★ _____

★ _____

★ _____

★ _____

★ _____

★ _____

★ _____

★ _____

★ _____

★ _____

★ _____

★ _____

★ _____

★ _____

★ _____

★ _____

★ _____

★ _____

Positive Affirmations For Money, Wealth And Abundance

- Money and wealth comes to me easily.
- I am attracting more and more money all the time.
- Money magically flows to me in new ways.
- I am open to new sources of income.
- My prosperity is always increasing.
- I am attracting increasing amounts of money every day.
- My prosperity is improving beyond what I can imagine.
- I allow and accept more and more money into my life.
- Money flows easily to me and I enjoy it.
- I have infinite abundance in my life now.
- I am a magnet for money.
- I am completely aligned with wealth and abundance.
- I am creating new opportunities for abundance now.
- I give and receive money easily and happily.
- I can easily pay all my bills and know I have plenty of money.
- I am well paid and I love my job.
- I am attracting new windfalls of money.
- I am a master of my own wealth.
- I am prosperous and wealthy now.
- I have positive beliefs around money and abundance.

- I am so grateful for all my money.
- The Universe provides me with a plentiful supply of money.
- I am rich in so many ways.
- I believe I am worthy of my increasing prosperity.
- I know money is flowing to me from many sources.
- It is easy for me to receive money.
- I have endless supplies of money and this is true.
- My bank account is full of money.
- I am ready, willing and able to accept more and more money flowing to me now.
- I have infinite sources of income.
- Money always has a positive influence on my life.
- I love myself completely and I know I am already wealthy.
- Money is providing me with happy, loving experiences.
- I welcome more and more money into my life and I am grateful.
- I love money and money loves me.
- I continuously attract money.
- I am always grateful for my income.
- I am successful, wealthy, happy and grateful.

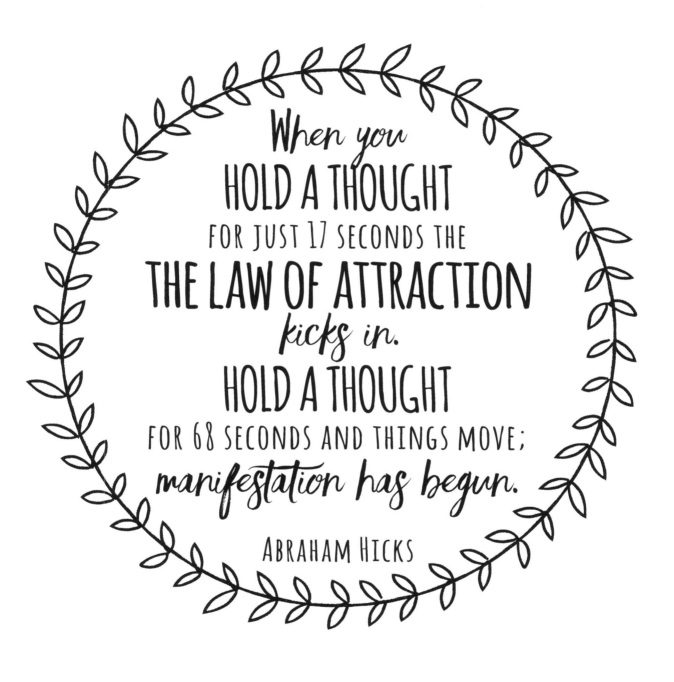

When you
HOLD A THOUGHT
FOR JUST 17 SECONDS THE
THE LAW OF ATTRACTION
kicks in.
HOLD A THOUGHT
FOR 68 SECONDS AND THINGS MOVE;
manifestation has begun.

ABRAHAM HICKS

MONEY MAGIC JOURNAL

Date:................

I SET MY INTENTION TO MANIFESTING:

VISUALISE ATTAINING THE GOAL. HOW DOES IT FEEL?

WHAT ACTION CAN I TAKE TOWARDS MY GOAL?

TODAY'S AFFIRMATION IS:

I AM GRATEFUL FOR:

MONEY MAGIC JOURNAL

Date:................

I SET MY INTENTION TO MANIFESTING:

_____
_____
_____
_____
_____

VISUALISE ATTAINING THE GOAL. HOW DOES IT FEEL?

_____
_____
_____
_____
_____

WHAT ACTION CAN I TAKE TOWARDS MY GOAL?

_____
_____
_____
_____

TODAY'S AFFIRMATION IS:

_____
_____

I AM GRATEFUL FOR:

_____
_____
_____
_____

MONEY MAGIC JOURNAL

Date:................

I SET MY INTENTION TO MANIFESTING:

VISUALISE ATTAINING THE GOAL. HOW DOES IT FEEL?

WHAT ACTION CAN I TAKE TOWARDS MY GOAL?

TODAY'S AFFIRMATION IS:

I AM GRATEFUL FOR:

MONEY MAGIC JOURNAL

Date: . . . .

I SET MY INTENTION TO MANIFESTING:

VISUALISE ATTAINING THE GOAL. HOW DOES IT FEEL?

WHAT ACTION CAN I TAKE TOWARDS MY GOAL?

TODAY'S AFFIRMATION IS:

I AM GRATEFUL FOR:

MONEY MAGIC JOURNAL

Date:..................

I SET MY INTENTION TO MANIFESTING:

VISUALISE ATTAINING THE GOAL. HOW DOES IT FEEL?

WHAT ACTION CAN I TAKE TOWARDS MY GOAL?

TODAY'S AFFIRMATION IS:

I AM GRATEFUL FOR:

MONEY MAGIC JOURNAL

Date:................

I SET MY INTENTION TO MANIFESTING:

VISUALISE ATTAINING THE GOAL. HOW DOES IT FEEL?

WHAT ACTION CAN I TAKE TOWARDS MY GOAL?

TODAY'S AFFIRMATION IS:

I AM GRATEFUL FOR:

MONEY MAGIC JOURNAL

Date:................

I SET MY INTENTION TO MANIFESTING:

VISUALISE ATTAINING THE GOAL. HOW DOES IT FEEL?

WHAT ACTION CAN I TAKE TOWARDS MY GOAL?

TODAY'S AFFIRMATION IS:

I AM GRATEFUL FOR:

MONEY MAGIC JOURNAL

Date:.................

I SET MY INTENTION TO MANIFESTING:

VISUALISE ATTAINING THE GOAL. HOW DOES IT FEEL?

WHAT ACTION CAN I TAKE TOWARDS MY GOAL?

TODAY'S AFFIRMATION IS:

I AM GRATEFUL FOR:

MONEY MAGIC JOURNAL

Date:................

I SET MY INTENTION TO MANIFESTING:

VISUALISE ATTAINING THE GOAL. HOW DOES IT FEEL?

WHAT ACTION CAN I TAKE TOWARDS MY GOAL?

TODAY'S AFFIRMATION IS:

I AM GRATEFUL FOR:

MONEY MAGIC JOURNAL

Date: . . . .

I SET MY INTENTION TO MANIFESTING:

VISUALISE ATTAINING THE GOAL. HOW DOES IT FEEL?

WHAT ACTION CAN I TAKE TOWARDS MY GOAL?

TODAY'S AFFIRMATION IS:

I AM GRATEFUL FOR:

MONEY MAGIC JOURNAL

Date:.................

I SET MY INTENTION TO MANIFESTING:

VISUALISE ATTAINING THE GOAL. HOW DOES IT FEEL?

WHAT ACTION CAN I TAKE TOWARDS MY GOAL?

TODAY'S AFFIRMATION IS:

I AM GRATEFUL FOR:

MONEY MAGIC JOURNAL

Date: . . . .

I SET MY INTENTION TO MANIFESTING:

VISUALISE ATTAINING THE GOAL. HOW DOES IT FEEL?

WHAT ACTION CAN I TAKE TOWARDS MY GOAL?

TODAY'S AFFIRMATION IS:

I AM GRATEFUL FOR:

MONEY MAGIC JOURNAL

Date:................

I SET MY INTENTION TO MANIFESTING:

VISUALISE ATTAINING THE GOAL. HOW DOES IT FEEL?

WHAT ACTION CAN I TAKE TOWARDS MY GOAL?

TODAY'S AFFIRMATION IS:

I AM GRATEFUL FOR:

MONEY MAGIC JOURNAL

Date:................

I SET MY INTENTION TO MANIFESTING:

VISUALISE ATTAINING THE GOAL. HOW DOES IT FEEL?

WHAT ACTION CAN I TAKE TOWARDS MY GOAL?

TODAY'S AFFIRMATION IS:

I AM GRATEFUL FOR:

MONEY MAGIC JOURNAL

Date: . . . .

I SET MY INTENTION TO MANIFESTING:

_____

_____

_____

_____

_____

VISUALISE ATTAINING THE GOAL. HOW DOES IT FEEL?

_____

_____

_____

_____

_____

_____

WHAT ACTION CAN I TAKE TOWARDS MY GOAL?

_____

_____

_____

_____

TODAY'S AFFIRMATION IS:

_____

_____

_____

I AM GRATEFUL FOR:

_____

_____

_____

_____

MONEY MAGIC JOURNAL

Date: . . . .

I SET MY INTENTION TO MANIFESTING:

VISUALISE ATTAINING THE GOAL. HOW DOES IT FEEL?

WHAT ACTION CAN I TAKE TOWARDS MY GOAL?

TODAY'S AFFIRMATION IS:

I AM GRATEFUL FOR:

MONEY MAGIC JOURNAL

Date:.................

I SET MY INTENTION TO MANIFESTING:

VISUALISE ATTAINING THE GOAL. HOW DOES IT FEEL?

WHAT ACTION CAN I TAKE TOWARDS MY GOAL?

TODAY'S AFFIRMATION IS:

I AM GRATEFUL FOR:

MONEY MAGIC JOURNAL

Date:................

I SET MY INTENTION TO MANIFESTING:

VISUALISE ATTAINING THE GOAL. HOW DOES IT FEEL?

WHAT ACTION CAN I TAKE TOWARDS MY GOAL?

TODAY'S AFFIRMATION IS:

I AM GRATEFUL FOR:

MONEY MAGIC JOURNAL

Date: . . . .

I SET MY INTENTION TO MANIFESTING:

VISUALISE ATTAINING THE GOAL. HOW DOES IT FEEL?

WHAT ACTION CAN I TAKE TOWARDS MY GOAL?

TODAY'S AFFIRMATION IS:

I AM GRATEFUL FOR:

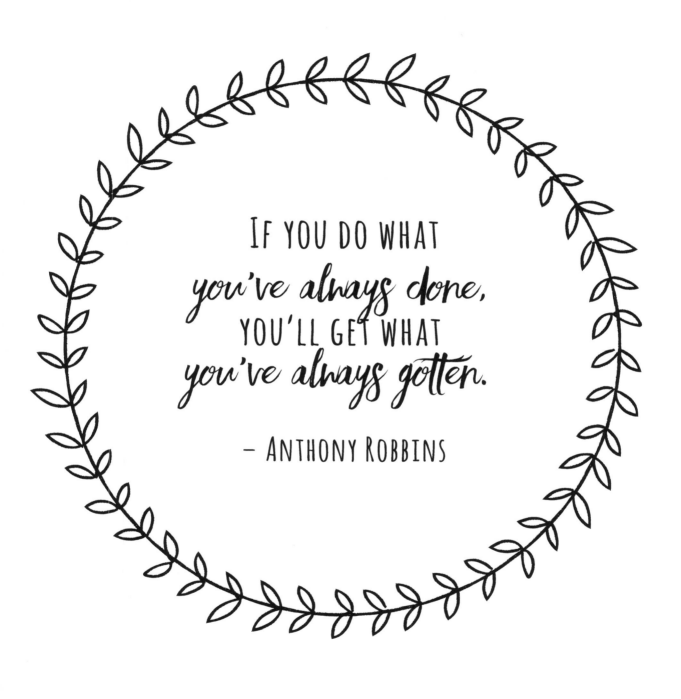

If you do what
you've always done,
you'll get what
you've always gotten.

– Anthony Robbins

MONEY MAGIC JOURNAL

Date:. . . . .

I SET MY INTENTION TO MANIFESTING:

VISUALISE ATTAINING THE GOAL. HOW DOES IT FEEL?

WHAT ACTION CAN I TAKE TOWARDS MY GOAL?

TODAY'S AFFIRMATION IS:

I AM GRATEFUL FOR:

MONEY MAGIC JOURNAL

Date: . . . .

I SET MY INTENTION TO MANIFESTING:

VISUALISE ATTAINING THE GOAL. HOW DOES IT FEEL?

WHAT ACTION CAN I TAKE TOWARDS MY GOAL?

TODAY'S AFFIRMATION IS:

I AM GRATEFUL FOR:

MONEY MAGIC JOURNAL

Date: . . . .

I SET MY INTENTION TO MANIFESTING:

VISUALISE ATTAINING THE GOAL. HOW DOES IT FEEL?

WHAT ACTION CAN I TAKE TOWARDS MY GOAL?

TODAY'S AFFIRMATION IS:

I AM GRATEFUL FOR:

MONEY MAGIC JOURNAL

Date:................

I SET MY INTENTION TO MANIFESTING:

_____

_____

_____

_____

_____

VISUALISE ATTAINING THE GOAL. HOW DOES IT FEEL?

_____

_____

_____

_____

_____

WHAT ACTION CAN I TAKE TOWARDS MY GOAL?

_____

_____

_____

_____

TODAY'S AFFIRMATION IS:

_____

_____

_____

I AM GRATEFUL FOR:

_____

_____

_____

_____

MONEY MAGIC JOURNAL

Date:...................

I SET MY INTENTION TO MANIFESTING:

VISUALISE ATTAINING THE GOAL. HOW DOES IT FEEL?

WHAT ACTION CAN I TAKE TOWARDS MY GOAL?

TODAY'S AFFIRMATION IS:

I AM GRATEFUL FOR:

MONEY MAGIC JOURNAL

Date:................

I SET MY INTENTION TO MANIFESTING:

VISUALISE ATTAINING THE GOAL. HOW DOES IT FEEL?

WHAT ACTION CAN I TAKE TOWARDS MY GOAL?

TODAY'S AFFIRMATION IS:

I AM GRATEFUL FOR:

MONEY MAGIC JOURNAL

Date: . . . .

I SET MY INTENTION TO MANIFESTING:

VISUALISE ATTAINING THE GOAL. HOW DOES IT FEEL?

WHAT ACTION CAN I TAKE TOWARDS MY GOAL?

TODAY'S AFFIRMATION IS:

I AM GRATEFUL FOR:

MONEY MAGIC JOURNAL

Date:..................

I SET MY INTENTION TO MANIFESTING:

VISUALISE ATTAINING THE GOAL. HOW DOES IT FEEL?

WHAT ACTION CAN I TAKE TOWARDS MY GOAL?

TODAY'S AFFIRMATION IS:

I AM GRATEFUL FOR:

MONEY MAGIC JOURNAL

Date: ....

I SET MY INTENTION TO MANIFESTING:

VISUALISE ATTAINING THE GOAL. HOW DOES IT FEEL?

WHAT ACTION CAN I TAKE TOWARDS MY GOAL?

TODAY'S AFFIRMATION IS:

I AM GRATEFUL FOR:

MONEY MAGIC JOURNAL

Date:................

I SET MY INTENTION TO MANIFESTING:

VISUALISE ATTAINING THE GOAL. HOW DOES IT FEEL?

WHAT ACTION CAN I TAKE TOWARDS MY GOAL?

TODAY'S AFFIRMATION IS:

I AM GRATEFUL FOR:

MONEY MAGIC JOURNAL

Date:. . . . .

I SET MY INTENTION TO MANIFESTING:

VISUALISE ATTAINING THE GOAL. HOW DOES IT FEEL?

WHAT ACTION CAN I TAKE TOWARDS MY GOAL?

TODAY'S AFFIRMATION IS:

I AM GRATEFUL FOR:

MONEY MAGIC JOURNAL

Date:................

I SET MY INTENTION TO MANIFESTING:

VISUALISE ATTAINING THE GOAL. HOW DOES IT FEEL?

WHAT ACTION CAN I TAKE TOWARDS MY GOAL?

TODAY'S AFFIRMATION IS:

I AM GRATEFUL FOR:

MONEY MAGIC JOURNAL

Date:.................

I SET MY INTENTION TO MANIFESTING:

VISUALISE ATTAINING THE GOAL. HOW DOES IT FEEL?

WHAT ACTION CAN I TAKE TOWARDS MY GOAL?

TODAY'S AFFIRMATION IS:

I AM GRATEFUL FOR:

MONEY MAGIC JOURNAL

Date:................

I SET MY INTENTION TO MANIFESTING:

_____
_____
_____
_____
_____

VISUALISE ATTAINING THE GOAL. HOW DOES IT FEEL?

_____
_____
_____
_____
_____

WHAT ACTION CAN I TAKE TOWARDS MY GOAL?

_____
_____
_____
_____

TODAY'S AFFIRMATION IS:

_____
_____
_____

I AM GRATEFUL FOR:

_____
_____
_____
_____

MONEY MAGIC JOURNAL

Date: . . . .

I SET MY INTENTION TO MANIFESTING:

VISUALISE ATTAINING THE GOAL. HOW DOES IT FEEL?

WHAT ACTION CAN I TAKE TOWARDS MY GOAL?

TODAY'S AFFIRMATION IS:

I AM GRATEFUL FOR:

MONEY MAGIC JOURNAL

Date:................

I SET MY INTENTION TO MANIFESTING:

VISUALISE ATTAINING THE GOAL. HOW DOES IT FEEL?

WHAT ACTION CAN I TAKE TOWARDS MY GOAL?

TODAY'S AFFIRMATION IS:

I AM GRATEFUL FOR:

MONEY MAGIC JOURNAL

Date: . . . .

I SET MY INTENTION TO MANIFESTING:

VISUALISE ATTAINING THE GOAL. HOW DOES IT FEEL?

WHAT ACTION CAN I TAKE TOWARDS MY GOAL?

TODAY'S AFFIRMATION IS:

I AM GRATEFUL FOR:

MONEY MAGIC JOURNAL

Date: . . . .

I SET MY INTENTION TO MANIFESTING:

VISUALISE ATTAINING THE GOAL. HOW DOES IT FEEL?

WHAT ACTION CAN I TAKE TOWARDS MY GOAL?

TODAY'S AFFIRMATION IS:

I AM GRATEFUL FOR:

MONEY MAGIC JOURNAL

Date:.................

I SET MY INTENTION TO MANIFESTING:

VISUALISE ATTAINING THE GOAL. HOW DOES IT FEEL?

WHAT ACTION CAN I TAKE TOWARDS MY GOAL?

TODAY'S AFFIRMATION IS:

I AM GRATEFUL FOR:

MONEY MAGIC JOURNAL

Date: . . . .

I SET MY INTENTION TO MANIFESTING:

VISUALISE ATTAINING THE GOAL. HOW DOES IT FEEL?

WHAT ACTION CAN I TAKE TOWARDS MY GOAL?

TODAY'S AFFIRMATION IS:

I AM GRATEFUL FOR:

MONEY MAGIC JOURNAL

Date:................

I SET MY INTENTION TO MANIFESTING:

VISUALISE ATTAINING THE GOAL. HOW DOES IT FEEL?

WHAT ACTION CAN I TAKE TOWARDS MY GOAL?

TODAY'S AFFIRMATION IS:

I AM GRATEFUL FOR:

MONEY MAGIC JOURNAL

I SET MY INTENTION TO MANIFESTING:

VISUALISE ATTAINING THE GOAL. HOW DOES IT FEEL?

WHAT ACTION CAN I TAKE TOWARDS MY GOAL?

TODAY'S AFFIRMATION IS:

I AM GRATEFUL FOR:

MONEY MAGIC JOURNAL

Date:................

I SET MY INTENTION TO MANIFESTING:

VISUALISE ATTAINING THE GOAL. HOW DOES IT FEEL?

WHAT ACTION CAN I TAKE TOWARDS MY GOAL?

TODAY'S AFFIRMATION IS:

I AM GRATEFUL FOR:

MONEY MAGIC JOURNAL

Date:.................

I SET MY INTENTION TO MANIFESTING:

VISUALISE ATTAINING THE GOAL. HOW DOES IT FEEL?

WHAT ACTION CAN I TAKE TOWARDS MY GOAL?

TODAY'S AFFIRMATION IS:

I AM GRATEFUL FOR:

MONEY MAGIC JOURNAL

Date:...............

I SET MY INTENTION TO MANIFESTING:

VISUALISE ATTAINING THE GOAL. HOW DOES IT FEEL?

WHAT ACTION CAN I TAKE TOWARDS MY GOAL?

TODAY'S AFFIRMATION IS:

I AM GRATEFUL FOR:

MONEY MAGIC JOURNAL

Date: . . . .

I SET MY INTENTION TO MANIFESTING:

_____
_____
_____
_____
_____
_____

VISUALISE ATTAINING THE GOAL. HOW DOES IT FEEL?

_____
_____
_____
_____
_____
_____

WHAT ACTION CAN I TAKE TOWARDS MY GOAL?

_____
_____
_____
_____

TODAY'S AFFIRMATION IS:

_____
_____
_____

I AM GRATEFUL FOR:

_____
_____
_____
_____

MONEY MAGIC JOURNAL

Date:................

I SET MY INTENTION TO MANIFESTING:

VISUALISE ATTAINING THE GOAL. HOW DOES IT FEEL?

WHAT ACTION CAN I TAKE TOWARDS MY GOAL?

TODAY'S AFFIRMATION IS:

I AM GRATEFUL FOR:

MONEY MAGIC JOURNAL

Date:.................

I SET MY INTENTION TO MANIFESTING:

VISUALISE ATTAINING THE GOAL. HOW DOES IT FEEL?

WHAT ACTION CAN I TAKE TOWARDS MY GOAL?

TODAY'S AFFIRMATION IS:

I AM GRATEFUL FOR:

MONEY MAGIC JOURNAL

Date:................

I SET MY INTENTION TO MANIFESTING:

VISUALISE ATTAINING THE GOAL. HOW DOES IT FEEL?

WHAT ACTION CAN I TAKE TOWARDS MY GOAL?

TODAY'S AFFIRMATION IS:

I AM GRATEFUL FOR:

Everything is energy
and that is all there is to it.
MATCH THE FREQUENCY OF THE
REALITY YOU WANT AND YOU CANNOT HELP
BUT GET THAT REALITY.
It can be no other way.
This is not philosophy.
THIS IS PHYSICS.

– ALBERT EINSTEIN

MONEY MAGIC JOURNAL

Date: . . . .

I SET MY INTENTION TO MANIFESTING:

VISUALISE ATTAINING THE GOAL. HOW DOES IT FEEL?

WHAT ACTION CAN I TAKE TOWARDS MY GOAL?

TODAY'S AFFIRMATION IS:

I AM GRATEFUL FOR:

MONEY MAGIC JOURNAL

Date: . . . .

I SET MY INTENTION TO MANIFESTING:

VISUALISE ATTAINING THE GOAL. HOW DOES IT FEEL?

WHAT ACTION CAN I TAKE TOWARDS MY GOAL?

TODAY'S AFFIRMATION IS:

I AM GRATEFUL FOR:

MONEY MAGIC JOURNAL

Date: . . . .

I SET MY INTENTION TO MANIFESTING:

VISUALISE ATTAINING THE GOAL. HOW DOES IT FEEL?

WHAT ACTION CAN I TAKE TOWARDS MY GOAL?

TODAY'S AFFIRMATION IS:

I AM GRATEFUL FOR:

MONEY MAGIC JOURNAL

Date: . . . .

I SET MY INTENTION TO MANIFESTING:

VISUALISE ATTAINING THE GOAL. HOW DOES IT FEEL?

WHAT ACTION CAN I TAKE TOWARDS MY GOAL?

TODAY'S AFFIRMATION IS:

I AM GRATEFUL FOR:

MONEY MAGIC JOURNAL

Date: . . . .

I SET MY INTENTION TO MANIFESTING:

VISUALISE ATTAINING THE GOAL. HOW DOES IT FEEL?

WHAT ACTION CAN I TAKE TOWARDS MY GOAL?

TODAY'S AFFIRMATION IS:

I AM GRATEFUL FOR:

MONEY MAGIC JOURNAL

Date: . . . .

I SET MY INTENTION TO MANIFESTING:

VISUALISE ATTAINING THE GOAL. HOW DOES IT FEEL?

WHAT ACTION CAN I TAKE TOWARDS MY GOAL?

TODAY'S AFFIRMATION IS:

I AM GRATEFUL FOR:

MONEY MAGIC JOURNAL

Date: . . . .

I SET MY INTENTION TO MANIFESTING:

VISUALISE ATTAINING THE GOAL. HOW DOES IT FEEL?

WHAT ACTION CAN I TAKE TOWARDS MY GOAL?

TODAY'S AFFIRMATION IS:

I AM GRATEFUL FOR:

MONEY MAGIC JOURNAL

Date:................

I SET MY INTENTION TO MANIFESTING:

VISUALISE ATTAINING THE GOAL. HOW DOES IT FEEL?

WHAT ACTION CAN I TAKE TOWARDS MY GOAL?

TODAY'S AFFIRMATION IS:

I AM GRATEFUL FOR:

MONEY MAGIC JOURNAL

Date:.................

I SET MY INTENTION TO MANIFESTING:

VISUALISE ATTAINING THE GOAL. HOW DOES IT FEEL?

WHAT ACTION CAN I TAKE TOWARDS MY GOAL?

TODAY'S AFFIRMATION IS:

I AM GRATEFUL FOR:

MONEY MAGIC JOURNAL

Date:..................

I SET MY INTENTION TO MANIFESTING:

VISUALISE ATTAINING THE GOAL. HOW DOES IT FEEL?

WHAT ACTION CAN I TAKE TOWARDS MY GOAL?

TODAY'S AFFIRMATION IS:

I AM GRATEFUL FOR:

MONEY MAGIC JOURNAL

Date:................

I SET MY INTENTION TO MANIFESTING:

VISUALISE ATTAINING THE GOAL. HOW DOES IT FEEL?

WHAT ACTION CAN I TAKE TOWARDS MY GOAL?

TODAY'S AFFIRMATION IS:

I AM GRATEFUL FOR:

MONEY MAGIC JOURNAL

Date:.................

I SET MY INTENTION TO MANIFESTING:

VISUALISE ATTAINING THE GOAL. HOW DOES IT FEEL?

WHAT ACTION CAN I TAKE TOWARDS MY GOAL?

TODAY'S AFFIRMATION IS:

I AM GRATEFUL FOR:

MONEY MAGIC JOURNAL

Date: . . . .

I SET MY INTENTION TO MANIFESTING:

VISUALISE ATTAINING THE GOAL. HOW DOES IT FEEL?

WHAT ACTION CAN I TAKE TOWARDS MY GOAL?

TODAY'S AFFIRMATION IS:

I AM GRATEFUL FOR:

MONEY MAGIC JOURNAL

I SET MY INTENTION TO MANIFESTING:

VISUALISE ATTAINING THE GOAL. HOW DOES IT FEEL?

WHAT ACTION CAN I TAKE TOWARDS MY GOAL?

TODAY'S AFFIRMATION IS:

I AM GRATEFUL FOR:

MONEY MAGIC JOURNAL

Date: . . . .

I SET MY INTENTION TO MANIFESTING:

_____

_____

_____

_____

_____

VISUALISE ATTAINING THE GOAL. HOW DOES IT FEEL?

_____

_____

_____

_____

_____

WHAT ACTION CAN I TAKE TOWARDS MY GOAL?

_____

_____

_____

_____

TODAY'S AFFIRMATION IS:

_____

_____

I AM GRATEFUL FOR:

_____

_____

_____

_____

MONEY MAGIC JOURNAL

Date: . . . .

I SET MY INTENTION TO MANIFESTING:

_____
_____
_____
_____
_____
_____

VISUALISE ATTAINING THE GOAL. HOW DOES IT FEEL?

_____
_____
_____
_____
_____
_____

WHAT ACTION CAN I TAKE TOWARDS MY GOAL?

_____
_____
_____
_____

TODAY'S AFFIRMATION IS:

_____
_____
_____

I AM GRATEFUL FOR:

_____
_____
_____
_____
_____

MONEY MAGIC JOURNAL

Date:................

I SET MY INTENTION TO MANIFESTING:

VISUALISE ATTAINING THE GOAL. HOW DOES IT FEEL?

WHAT ACTION CAN I TAKE TOWARDS MY GOAL?

TODAY'S AFFIRMATION IS:

I AM GRATEFUL FOR:

MONEY MAGIC JOURNAL

Date: . . . .

I SET MY INTENTION TO MANIFESTING:

VISUALISE ATTAINING THE GOAL. HOW DOES IT FEEL?

WHAT ACTION CAN I TAKE TOWARDS MY GOAL?

TODAY'S AFFIRMATION IS:

I AM GRATEFUL FOR:

MONEY MAGIC JOURNAL

Date:................

I SET MY INTENTION TO MANIFESTING:

VISUALISE ATTAINING THE GOAL. HOW DOES IT FEEL?

WHAT ACTION CAN I TAKE TOWARDS MY GOAL?

TODAY'S AFFIRMATION IS:

I AM GRATEFUL FOR:

MONEY MAGIC JOURNAL

Date:................

I SET MY INTENTION TO MANIFESTING:

_____

_____

_____

_____

_____

VISUALISE ATTAINING THE GOAL. HOW DOES IT FEEL?

_____

_____

_____

_____

_____

WHAT ACTION CAN I TAKE TOWARDS MY GOAL?

_____

_____

_____

_____

TODAY'S AFFIRMATION IS:

_____

_____

_____

I AM GRATEFUL FOR:

_____

_____

_____

_____

MONEY MAGIC JOURNAL

Date: . . . .

I SET MY INTENTION TO MANIFESTING:

VISUALISE ATTAINING THE GOAL. HOW DOES IT FEEL?

WHAT ACTION CAN I TAKE TOWARDS MY GOAL?

TODAY'S AFFIRMATION IS:

I AM GRATEFUL FOR:

MONEY MAGIC JOURNAL

Date:................

I SET MY INTENTION TO MANIFESTING:

_____
_____
_____
_____
_____
_____

VISUALISE ATTAINING THE GOAL. HOW DOES IT FEEL?

_____
_____
_____
_____
_____
_____

WHAT ACTION CAN I TAKE TOWARDS MY GOAL?

_____
_____
_____
_____
_____

TODAY'S AFFIRMATION IS:

_____
_____
_____

I AM GRATEFUL FOR:

_____
_____
_____
_____
_____

MONEY MAGIC JOURNAL

Date:..................

I SET MY INTENTION TO MANIFESTING:

VISUALISE ATTAINING THE GOAL. HOW DOES IT FEEL?

WHAT ACTION CAN I TAKE TOWARDS MY GOAL?

TODAY'S AFFIRMATION IS:

I AM GRATEFUL FOR:

MONEY MAGIC JOURNAL

Date: . . . .

I SET MY INTENTION TO MANIFESTING:

VISUALISE ATTAINING THE GOAL. HOW DOES IT FEEL?

WHAT ACTION CAN I TAKE TOWARDS MY GOAL?

TODAY'S AFFIRMATION IS:

I AM GRATEFUL FOR:

MONEY MAGIC JOURNAL

Date: . . . .

I SET MY INTENTION TO MANIFESTING:

VISUALISE ATTAINING THE GOAL. HOW DOES IT FEEL?

WHAT ACTION CAN I TAKE TOWARDS MY GOAL?

TODAY'S AFFIRMATION IS:

I AM GRATEFUL FOR:

MONEY MAGIC JOURNAL

Date:................

I SET MY INTENTION TO MANIFESTING:

VISUALISE ATTAINING THE GOAL. HOW DOES IT FEEL?

WHAT ACTION CAN I TAKE TOWARDS MY GOAL?

TODAY'S AFFIRMATION IS:

I AM GRATEFUL FOR:

MONEY MAGIC JOURNAL

Date:...............

I SET MY INTENTION TO MANIFESTING:

VISUALISE ATTAINING THE GOAL. HOW DOES IT FEEL?

WHAT ACTION CAN I TAKE TOWARDS MY GOAL?

TODAY'S AFFIRMATION IS:

I AM GRATEFUL FOR:

MONEY MAGIC JOURNAL

Date:................

I SET MY INTENTION TO MANIFESTING:

VISUALISE ATTAINING THE GOAL. HOW DOES IT FEEL?

WHAT ACTION CAN I TAKE TOWARDS MY GOAL?

TODAY'S AFFIRMATION IS:

I AM GRATEFUL FOR:

MONEY MAGIC JOURNAL

Date:..................

I SET MY INTENTION TO MANIFESTING:

VISUALISE ATTAINING THE GOAL. HOW DOES IT FEEL?

WHAT ACTION CAN I TAKE TOWARDS MY GOAL?

TODAY'S AFFIRMATION IS:

I AM GRATEFUL FOR:

MONEY MAGIC JOURNAL

Date:................

I SET MY INTENTION TO MANIFESTING:

VISUALISE ATTAINING THE GOAL. HOW DOES IT FEEL?

WHAT ACTION CAN I TAKE TOWARDS MY GOAL?

TODAY'S AFFIRMATION IS:

I AM GRATEFUL FOR:

MONEY MAGIC JOURNAL

Date: . . . .

I SET MY INTENTION TO MANIFESTING:

VISUALISE ATTAINING THE GOAL. HOW DOES IT FEEL?

WHAT ACTION CAN I TAKE TOWARDS MY GOAL?

TODAY'S AFFIRMATION IS:

I AM GRATEFUL FOR:

MONEY MAGIC JOURNAL

Date:. . . . .

I SET MY INTENTION TO MANIFESTING:

VISUALISE ATTAINING THE GOAL. HOW DOES IT FEEL?

WHAT ACTION CAN I TAKE TOWARDS MY GOAL?

TODAY'S AFFIRMATION IS:

I AM GRATEFUL FOR:

MONEY MAGIC JOURNAL

Date:.................

I SET MY INTENTION TO MANIFESTING:

VISUALISE ATTAINING THE GOAL. HOW DOES IT FEEL?

WHAT ACTION CAN I TAKE TOWARDS MY GOAL?

TODAY'S AFFIRMATION IS:

I AM GRATEFUL FOR:

MONEY MAGIC JOURNAL

Date:..................

I SET MY INTENTION TO MANIFESTING:

VISUALISE ATTAINING THE GOAL. HOW DOES IT FEEL?

WHAT ACTION CAN I TAKE TOWARDS MY GOAL?

TODAY'S AFFIRMATION IS:

I AM GRATEFUL FOR:

MONEY MAGIC JOURNAL

Date:. . . . .

I SET MY INTENTION TO MANIFESTING:

VISUALISE ATTAINING THE GOAL. HOW DOES IT FEEL?

WHAT ACTION CAN I TAKE TOWARDS MY GOAL?

TODAY'S AFFIRMATION IS:

I AM GRATEFUL FOR:

MONEY MAGIC JOURNAL

Date:................

I SET MY INTENTION TO MANIFESTING:

VISUALISE ATTAINING THE GOAL. HOW DOES IT FEEL?

WHAT ACTION CAN I TAKE TOWARDS MY GOAL?

TODAY'S AFFIRMATION IS:

I AM GRATEFUL FOR:

MONEY MAGIC JOURNAL

Date: . . . .

I SET MY INTENTION TO MANIFESTING:

VISUALISE ATTAINING THE GOAL. HOW DOES IT FEEL?

WHAT ACTION CAN I TAKE TOWARDS MY GOAL?

TODAY'S AFFIRMATION IS:

I AM GRATEFUL FOR:

MONEY MAGIC JOURNAL

Date:.................

I SET MY INTENTION TO MANIFESTING:

VISUALISE ATTAINING THE GOAL. HOW DOES IT FEEL?

WHAT ACTION CAN I TAKE TOWARDS MY GOAL?

TODAY'S AFFIRMATION IS:

I AM GRATEFUL FOR:

MONEY MAGIC JOURNAL

Date: . . . .

I SET MY INTENTION TO MANIFESTING:

VISUALISE ATTAINING THE GOAL. HOW DOES IT FEEL?

WHAT ACTION CAN I TAKE TOWARDS MY GOAL?

TODAY'S AFFIRMATION IS:

I AM GRATEFUL FOR:

MONEY MAGIC JOURNAL

Date: . . . .

I SET MY INTENTION TO MANIFESTING:

VISUALISE ATTAINING THE GOAL. HOW DOES IT FEEL?

WHAT ACTION CAN I TAKE TOWARDS MY GOAL?

TODAY'S AFFIRMATION IS:

I AM GRATEFUL FOR:

MONEY MAGIC JOURNAL

Date:.................

I SET MY INTENTION TO MANIFESTING:

_____
_____
_____
_____
_____
_____

VISUALISE ATTAINING THE GOAL. HOW DOES IT FEEL?

_____
_____
_____
_____
_____
_____

WHAT ACTION CAN I TAKE TOWARDS MY GOAL?

_____
_____
_____
_____

TODAY'S AFFIRMATION IS:

_____
_____
_____

I AM GRATEFUL FOR:

_____
_____
_____
_____

MONEY MAGIC JOURNAL

Date: . . . .

I SET MY INTENTION TO MANIFESTING:

VISUALISE ATTAINING THE GOAL. HOW DOES IT FEEL?

WHAT ACTION CAN I TAKE TOWARDS MY GOAL?

TODAY'S AFFIRMATION IS:

I AM GRATEFUL FOR:

MONEY MAGIC JOURNAL

Date:................

I SET MY INTENTION TO MANIFESTING:

VISUALISE ATTAINING THE GOAL. HOW DOES IT FEEL?

WHAT ACTION CAN I TAKE TOWARDS MY GOAL?

TODAY'S AFFIRMATION IS:

I AM GRATEFUL FOR:

MONEY MAGIC JOURNAL

Date:.................

I SET MY INTENTION TO MANIFESTING:

VISUALISE ATTAINING THE GOAL. HOW DOES IT FEEL?

WHAT ACTION CAN I TAKE TOWARDS MY GOAL?

TODAY'S AFFIRMATION IS:

I AM GRATEFUL FOR:

33491659R00060

Printed in Poland
by Amazon Fulfillment
Poland Sp. z o.o., Wrocław